games handbook

PARTY GAMES!

Lisa Regan

QED

QED Publishing

Editor: Sarah Eason
Designer: Calcium
Illustrators: Owen Rimington and Emma DeBanks

Copyright © QED Publishing 2010

First published in the UK in 2010 by
QED Publishing
A Quarto Group company
226 City Road
London EC1V 2TT

www.qed-publishing.co.uk

A catalogue record for this book is available
from the British Library.

ISBN 978 1 84835 458 6

Printed in China

CONTENTS

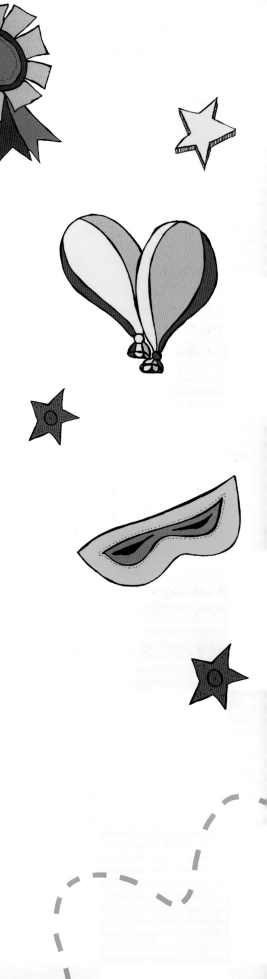

How to Use this Book 4

Who's Gone? 6

The Zoo Game 7

Cartoon Time 8

Balloon Darts 9

Pop Go the Prizes 10

Strawberries and Cream 11

Balloons Away! 12

Aeroplanes 13

Ghost Hunting 14

Squeak, Piggy, Squeak! 15

Party Pins 16

Rush Hour 17

Musical Mayhem 18

Sleeping Lions 20

Post Box 21

Tray Hard 22

In the Bag 23

Spoon Wars 24

Bonk! 25

Slip Slop 26

Frustration 27

Human Chain 28

The Name Game 29

Simon Says 30

Spider's Web 31

Drama School 32

HOW TO USE THIS BOOK

Gather all your friends around, let's get this party off the ground!

Hurray! It's party time! Whether you are having a party at home for a few friends, or a party in a big hall with lots of people, you will need some games to play! This book has plenty to choose from – racing games, games with prizes, games just for fun, and quieter games to calm things down. There is also a whole heap of games you can play at family parties – get your granny and your cousins to join in the fun!

You will need

All the games tell you what you need to be able to play. Some of them need some advance preparation, so you don't waste precious party time setting things up. Others need a few easy-to-find items from around your home. Lots of them just need music and your friends.

4

Difficulty

No one wants to stand around listening to complicated instructions – everyone just wants to play! So the games in this book are all quite simple to understand. Some of them are easy peasy, some of them demand more skill. The easiest games are marked with * and are at the beginning of the book. The hardest games are at the end, marked * * * * *, and the games in between are – well, in between!

SIMON SAYS

You will need:
• grown-up to lead

If Simon says it, you must do it, but don't be fooled – he'll trick you to it!

Difficulty: ⭐⭐⭐⭐⭐   Players: any number

1 All the players watch the grown-up at the front of the room. They give out instructions such as, "pat your head", "run on the spot" or "stick out your tongue".

2 The players must only follow the instruction if the grown-up has said, "Simon says…" before the action.

3 Anyone who gets it wrong, by doing the action when the grown-up did not say "Simon says" first, or not doing the action that Simon said, is out.

The winner is… the last person doing exactly what Simon says, without slipping up.

Did You Know?
'Simon Says' was made into an electronic game that flashed coloured lights in order. Players had to remember which order the lights flashed in.

30

SPIDER'S WEB

You will need:
• lots of balls of wool
• small presents

This spider's web game is great fun, climb in and out with everyone.

Difficulty: ⭐⭐⭐⭐⭐   Players: any number

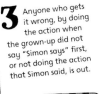

1 Prepare this game before the party starts. Tie one end of a ball of wool to each small present – one per player. Hide the presents.

2 Unwind each ball of wool around table legs, door handles, staircases and so on, to make a giant criss-crossed spider's web.

3 As the guests arrive, give each of them the end of one ball of wool. They have to crawl in and out of the web, under furniture and around each other, winding up their wool as they go, to get to their prize.

Bet You Can't!
tie different coloured lengths of wool together, so that each person's start and finish colour is different – there can be no cheating that way!

The winner is… everyone who finds their present!

31

Did You Know?

For some games you will find fascinating facts related to them, to add to the fun.

Bet You Can't!

Is everyone just too good already? Do you want to add an extra, more challenging twist to some of the games to make people earn their prizes? Read this section and see how to make things harder, or just funnier!

5

WHO'S GONE?

**Lots of people – one has gone,
look around and guess which one.**

Difficulty: ⭐ **Players:** everyone at the party

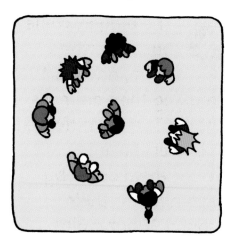

2 One person leaves the room, and the others close up the gap in the circle. The player in the middle must open their eyes and say who is missing.

3 Don't worry if you don't know everyone's name. You can simply describe the missing person by what they are wearing, or by the colour of their hair.

1 Stand in a big circle, with one player in the middle. They have to look around the circle to remember who is there, then they close their eyes.

Bet You Can't!
Make the game harder by making two people swap places, instead of leaving the room. The person in the middle must guess who has swapped round.

The winner is...
no one, but it's a great first game for getting to know everyone.

You will need:
....
• just yourselves

THE ZOO GAME

Find your partner by their growl, lots of animals on the prowl!

Difficulty: ⭐ **Players:** an equal number split into pairs

You will need:
....
• scarves for blindfolds

2 One person from each pair leaves the room. The others are all blindfolded.

3 The players come back into the room, and start making their animal's noise. Their blindfolded partners have to track them down by listening for their sound. What a din!

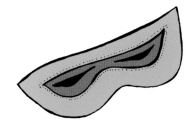

1 Each pair of players chooses an animal that makes a cool noise. Think about a lion's roar, an owl's hoot or a pig's snort.

Did You Know?

Chimpanzees are the noisiest apes. They make about a dozen different noises, including hooting, screeching and whimpering.

The winner is... the first pair to meet up — but really it's just an excuse for being really noisy!

CARTOON TIME

Grab your paper and a pen. Search high and low to find Ben 10!

Difficulty: ⭐ **Players:** any number

You will need:
....
- about 12 pictures of cartoon characters
- pencils
- paper
- sticky putty

2 Each player has an answer sheet with all the pictures on it, and space to write the number from each picture alongside.

3 As you find each character, write down the number in the correct space on your answer sheet.

1 Write a number on each picture of a cartoon character, then put them up around the home. Stick them to the fridge, behind a door or inside a cupboard.

The winner is... the first person to find all the pictures and write down the correct numbers.

Did You Know?

Scooby Doo has been around since 1969 — which means the characters should look older than your mum or dad by now!

BALLOON DARTS

Blow it up and let it go, will your score be high or low?

Difficulty: ⭐ **Players:** any number

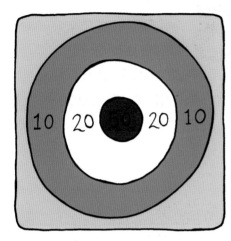

10 20 50 20 10

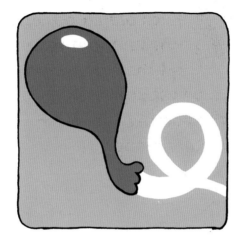

3 Keep the score if anyone's balloon actually lands on the target!

1 Draw a target on a big piece of paper. Give it two rings and a centre 'bull's-eye' circle. Colour it in like the one above. Write '10' in the outer ring, '20' in the second ring and '50' in the bull's-eye. Place the target in the middle of the floor.

2 Each player has a balloon. They stand in a row. They take it in turns to blow up their balloon a little bit and then let go, aiming for the target.

The winner is...
the person with the highest score after three turns each.

Did You Know?
A real dartboard has the scores 1 to 20 on it, but for this game it is better to have fewer, bigger spaces with just three scores.

POP GO THE PRIZES

Bursting balloons is really fun, pop each one, see what you've won!

Difficulty: ⭐ **Players:** any number

You will need:
....
- pencils
- paper
- balloons
- small prizes

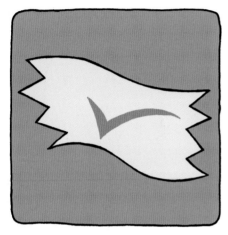

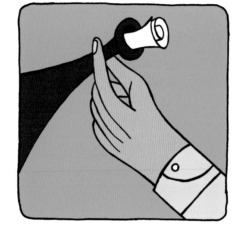

3 At the party, release all the balloons at once and get everyone to jump on them! Pop a balloon and see if you have won a prize!

1 Before the party, prepare the balloons. Write messages on small pieces of paper. Your messages can simply say 'Prize!' or 'Sorry!'.

2 Blow up each balloon a little, then put a message inside. Finish blowing it up, and tie the knot.

The winner is... anyone who has a 'Prize!' message at the end of the game — they get a small prize.

Bet You Can't!
Write forfeits on some of the messages, to make people do funny things such as tell a joke or do a handstand.

STRAWBERRIES AND CREAM

Cover up your party dress,
this game will get you in a mess!

Difficulty: ⭐⭐ **Players:** any number

1 Put a strawberry on the plate and squirt some cream on top of it.

2 Cover the surrounding area – this could get messy!

3 Each player takes a turn to place their hands behind their back, and use only their mouth to try to eat the strawberry. Put out a new strawberry and cream for each player.

Bet You Can't!
Straight afterwards, see who can eat a sweet placed at the bottom of a bowl of cereal, again using only their mouth — the cream will make the cereal stick to their face!

The winner is...
everyone who manages to eat their strawberry!

11

BALLOONS AWAY!

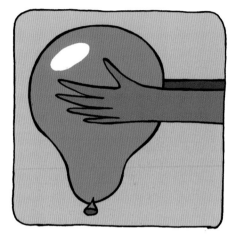

You will need:
....
• balloon

Catch the balloon before it drops, beat your friends and you'll be tops!

Difficulty: ⭐⭐   **Players:** 4 or more

1 Everyone stands in a circle. Each player is given a number to remember.

2 One person stands in the middle, holding up the balloon. They shout out a number, and throw or drop the balloon.

3 The person with that number must try to catch the balloon before it touches the ground.

Bet You Can't!
Call out two numbers each time — don't crash as you race to catch the balloon!

The winner is...
any player who catches the balloon in time — they can have a small prize.

AEROPLANES

Use your breath to blow your plane.
It helps to be windy for this game!

Difficulty: ⭐⭐ **Players:** 2 equal teams of at least 3 players

You will need:
....
- long pieces of string
- paper cups

1 Two players from each team hold the ends of their long piece of string, so that it is stretched across the room.

2 Make a small hole in the bottom of each paper cup, and thread one cup onto each string. Position it at one end.

3 The teams race against each other, with one player blowing into the open end of the cup to move it along the string. Keeping the string tight helps the cup to move faster. Swap round, so that everyone has a turn at holding the string and at blowing.

The winner is... the first team to finish, after all the players have had a turn at blowing.

Did You Know?

The fastest plane in the world is the Lockheed SR-71 Blackbird. It can fly at more than 1200 kilometres per hour. That would take some blowing!

GHOST HUNTING

Who's the ghost that's haunting you?
Give them a squeeze – they might go "Boo!"

You will need:
....
- pencils
- paper
- bed sheets (white if possible)

Difficulty: ⭐⭐ **Players:** 6 or more

2 Invite the other players back into the room. They have to guess who each ghost is. They write down their number and the name of who they think it is.

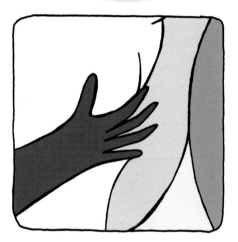

1 Half the players leave the room. The others are given a sheet each, to cover themselves like ghosts. Stick a number to each 'ghost'.

Bet You Can't!
Play this game in the dark, if the grown-ups will let you – the ghosts can chase the other players!

3 The people guessing can feel through the sheet, but they must not ask the ghost to speak, or poke them too hard!

The winner is...
the best guesser – but really it's just for fun.

14

SQUEAK, PIGGY, SQUEAK!

You will need:
....
- scarf for a blindfold

Put on the blindfold – you mustn't peek.
See if you recognize that squeak!

Difficulty: ⭐⭐ **Players:** 6 or more

3 The farmer says, "Squeak, piggy, squeak!" The person must squeak, so the farmer can try to guess who they are.

1 The players sit in a circle, on chairs or on the floor. One player stands in the middle and is blindfolded. They are the 'farmer'.

2 Twist the farmer around three times, and then let them find someone in the circle. They must sit on that person's knee.

The winner is...
no one, but each player takes a turn as the 'farmer'.

Did You Know?
This game is sometimes called 'Poor Pussy'. In that version, the blindfolded person is stroked like a cat!

PARTY PINS

The pirate's patch is on his ear.
A good attempt, you're very near!

Difficulty: ⭐⭐ **Players:** any number

You will need:
....
- large piece of paper
- pens
- sticky putty
- scarf for a blindfold
- items relating to the theme (see below)

1 Draw a large picture to match the theme of your party – for example, a pirate or a princess. Stick it to the wall using sticky putty.

2 The first player is blindfolded, placed one step away from the picture and given an item to stick onto the picture – such as an eye patch or an earring.

3 The blindfolded player sticks the item onto the picture where they think it should be. Write each player's name next to their effort, and make sure everyone has a turn.

Did You Know?
This game is traditionally called 'Pin the Tail on the Donkey'. Players have to pin a piece of string as close as possible to the donkey's bottom.

The winner is...
the person to stick the eye patch closest to the eye, or the earring closest to the ear. You will get some funny results!

RUSH HOUR

Racing round from town to town,
rush across and then sit down.

Difficulty: ⭐⭐ **Players:** 6 or more

You will need:
....
- one chair per player
- scarf for a blindfold

1 Arrange the chairs in a circle. All the players except one sit down. These players then choose the name of a town or city. One player stands in the middle of the circle, blindfolded.

2 A grown-up calls out the names of two of the towns. Those players have to run across the circle and swap seats, without being caught by the blindfolded player.

3 Sometimes the grown-up calls out "Rush hour!", and then everyone has to find a new seat without being caught! If you are caught, take a turn in the middle.

The winner is... anyone who doesn't get caught at all.

Did You Know?
Do not choose Bangkok in Thailand or Beijing in China as your city — they have some of the worst traffic jams in the world!

MUSICAL MAYHEM

Dance around with jumps and hops, don't be out when the music stops!

Difficulty: ⭐⭐ **Players:** the more the better

1 There are several musical games you can play that are all quite similar. Four of them are explained here.

2 In each version, a person (usually a grown-up) takes charge of the music. They play it for a short time and then stop it, or turn down the volume so it cannot be heard.

3 The grown-up decides who is 'out' and then turns the music back on for the next go.

The winner is... the last person remaining in the game when everyone else is out.

Did You Know?

In Russian, 'Musical chairs' is actually called 'It's boring sitting like this'!

18

Musical Chairs

Start with a practice round. Place one chair for each player in a line down the middle of the room. Put them so that half are facing one way and half the other way, alternately. The players must walk around and around the row of chairs. When the music stops, they must sit on a chair. After the practice round, take away one chair each time the music stops. The player who cannot sit down is out.

Did You Know?

In several countries, 'Musical chairs' is still known by its original name, 'Trip to Jerusalem'.

Musical Mats

Play in the same way as musical chairs, but with mats scattered around the floor. Take away one mat each time, to get a player out.

Musical Statues

This time, the players dance and jump in time to the music. When it stops, they must freeze like a statue. Anyone caught moving is out.

Musical Bumps

As with musical statues, players dance around until the music stops. Then they must sit on the floor as fast as they can. The last person to bump down is out.

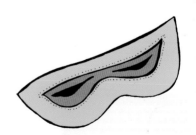

SLEEPING LIONS

A peaceful game to make you rest,
the stillest, quietest is the best.

Difficulty: ⭐⭐⭐ **Players:** any number

You will need:
....
- plenty of floor space

1 Grown-ups love this game, because everyone goes very still and quiet!

2 The rules are easy. Everyone lies on the floor and does not move. At all. Only breathing is allowed.

3 One person walks around the room looking for anyone who is sneakily giggling or twitching. Anyone even blinking is out!

The winner is... the last person lying perfectly still.

Bet You Can't!
Try to make the last ones in laugh, wriggle or look up if the game drags on for too long.

POST BOX

Pick up letters and post them in,
your gloves are fat but the slot is thin!

Difficulty: ⭐⭐⭐   **Players:** 2 equal teams

You will need:
....
- paper
- two boxes
- pair of mittens or oven gloves

2 Each team member takes a turn to put on the mittens, race to the end, collect a letter, then run back and post it in the post box.

3 If you like, you can write forfeits on each letter for the teams to do after the race has finished.

1 Turn the boxes upside down and cut a narrow slit in the top, to make a 'post box' for each team. Place a pile of pieces of paper, the 'letters', at the end of the course. Place the post box and the mittens at the beginning of the course.

The winner is...
the team with the most letters in their post box after a set time.

Did You Know?
More than 20 billion letters are posted every year in the UK — it's lucky the postal workers don't have to handle them all wearing mittens!

TRAY HARD

Remember what is on the tray,
then look to see what's gone away.

Difficulty: ★ ★ ★   **Players:** any number

You will need:
....
- tray
- about 20 small items (see below)
- tea towel

2 The players have 30 seconds to look at the tray and try to remember all the items on it.

1 Place about 20 small items on the tray, such as a key, an eraser, a whistle, a pen, a coin and a bouncy ball.

Bet You Can't!
Try to write down every item you remember from the tray. You win a small prize for each item you list correctly.

3 The tray is covered up, and one item is taken away. Then it is uncovered, and the players look again. They have to say which item is missing.

The winner is...
anyone who correctly names the missing item. If they get it right three times they win a small prize.

22

IN THE BAG

What items do these bags all hide?
It's hard to tell just what's inside.

Difficulty: ⭐⭐⭐ **Players:** any number

You will need:
- six paper bags
- small items (see below)
- pencils
- paper

1 Before the party, write a number on each paper bag. Place a different item in each bag. Use objects such as a highlighter pen, a fork, a hairclip, a toy car or a mobile phone.

2 The players must put their hand in each bag, and try to guess what is inside just by feeling it – they mustn't look!

3 Players can write or draw what they think is in each bag, or just whisper their answers to a grown-up.

The winner is... the person with the most correct answers on their list.

Did You Know?
Be careful what you put in the bags — some of the first toy cars ever made are now valuable. They can be worth more than £5000!

23

SPOON WARS

It's your ball they're all aiming for.
You'd better watch out – this is war!

Difficulty: ★ ★ ★ **Players:** any number

You will need:
- spoons
- bouncy balls

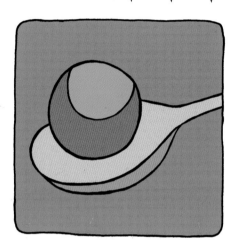

1 Everyone balances a bouncy ball on a spoon, just as you would in an egg-and-spoon race. You put your other hand behind your back.

2 You must move around the room, protecting your ball from being knocked off the spoon.

3 At the same time, you can try to knock off another player's ball. You decide whether you want to defend or attack!

The winner is... the last person to lose their ball from their spoon. Sit to the side if your ball falls off.

Did You Know?
Ashrita Furman of the United States ran one mile in 8 minutes and 25 seconds, holding an egg-and-spoon with both hands!

BONK!

Everyone follows the word that led.
Be quick to avoid a bonk on the head!

Difficulty: ⭐ ⭐ ⭐ **Players:** any number

You will need:
....
• soft object (such as a cuddly toy or a cushion)

1 This is a word game. Everyone sits round in a circle.

2 The first player says any word they think of. The next player has to quickly think of a word that is connected to that one. For example, if the first player says, "fish", the next player might say "chips". The sequence of words round the circle might then go like this: peas – green – blue – sky, and so on.

3 Any player who repeats a word, or hesitates too long, gets a gentle 'bonk' on the head with the soft item of your choice.

Did You Know?

Do not play this game with Frenchman Lluis Colet — he has twice held the world record for talking! In 2009, he spoke for five days and four nights non-stop (that's 124 hours!) about random subjects.

The winner is...

no one really — just try to avoid getting bonked on the head for as long as possible!

SLIP SLOP

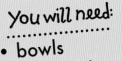

This game is full of slime and goo,
who will drop things – will it be you?

Difficulty: ⭐⭐⭐   **Players:** 2 equal teams

2 When the item reaches the end of the row, pass it back again – behind your backs! Put it in your 'finish' bowl.

3 Make sure you play this game outdoors, or wipe the floor when you have finished, to prevent any accidents!

1 Each team lines up, with its players standing side by side in a row. One player from each team races to the bowl and takes a slippery item. They must pass it from person to person down the line.

The winner is...
the team to pass all their items successfully and get them all into the 'finish' bowl.

Bet You Can't!
Play with more than one item moving at once, so that the players have to keep swapping their hands from back to front.

FRUSTRATION

Shaking six is quite a feat –
how much chocolate will you eat?

Difficulty: ⭐⭐⭐⭐ **Players:** any number

You will need:
....
- die
- fork and blunt knife
- big chocolate bar
- hat, scarf and gloves

1 Take it in turns to throw the die. You are trying to throw a six. The first person to throw a six runs to put on the clothes, then tries to cut a piece of chocolate from the bar with the knife and fork.

2 Meanwhile, the other players carry on rolling the die. If a six is thrown, that player must take the clothes off the first player and try to cut up some chocolate instead.

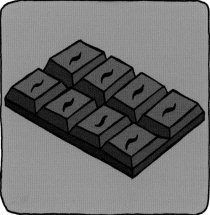

3 Keep changing players every time someone throws a six. There is no guarantee you will get any chocolate – quick throwing means quick changing!

Bet You Can't!
Start with the wrapper still on the chocolate bar, so the first player has to unwrap it wearing their gloves. So frustrating!

The winner is... no one, but hopefully everyone will get a taste of the chocolate.

27

HUMAN CHAIN

You will need:
....
• two hula hoops

Climb through the hoop as you stand in line. Which team will have the fastest time?

Difficulty: ⭐⭐⭐⭐ **Players:** 2 equal teams

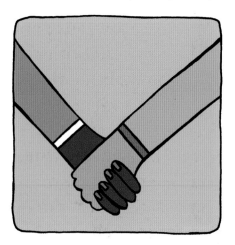 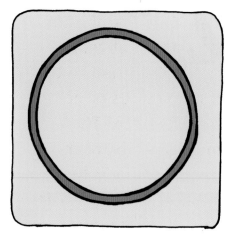 

1 The two teams stand in rows, holding hands with their team mates to form a chain.

2 Give the first player on each team a hula hoop. The aim is to pass the hoop along the chain, without breaking hands.

3 Step in and out of the hoop, wiggle and jiggle around, and use your knees and elbows to move it along – whatever it takes!

Did You Know?

This game would be easy with the world's biggest hula hoop — it measures 4.8 metres across. One man has even managed to spin it around his waist!

The winner is... the first team to get their hoop to the opposite end of their line.

THE NAME GAME

Describe the people from TV,
don't use their name, say what you see!

Difficulty: ⭐⭐⭐⭐ **Players:** 2 equal teams

You will need:
- scissors
- magazines
- box
- clock

1 Cut out pictures of famous people from magazines. For older players, just write their names on pieces of paper. Place them all in a box.

2 One member of the first team has a minute to take pictures or names from the box. They must describe as many people to their team as possible, so that their team mates guess who they are talking about.

3 You cannot say any of the celebrities' names, but you can say things such as, "He lives in Lazytown and has a funny moustache." Keep every picture or name that your team guesses correctly.

Bet You Can't!
Don't allow anyone to 'pass' — you have to keep guessing until your time runs out.

The winner is...
the team with the most pictures or names once the bag is empty.

SIMON SAYS

If Simon says it, you must do it,
but don't be fooled – he'll trick you to it!

Difficulty: ★★★★ **Players:** any number

You will need:
....
• grown-up to lead

1 All the players watch the grown-up at the front of the room. They give out instructions such as, "pat your head", "run on the spot" or "stick out your tongue".

2 The players must only follow the instruction if the grown-up has said, "Simon says…" before the action.

3 Anyone who gets it wrong, by doing the action when the grown-up did not say "Simon says" first, or not doing the action that Simon said, is out.

The winner is… the last person doing exactly what Simon says, without slipping up.

Did You Know?

'Simon Says' was made into an electronic game that flashed coloured lights in order. Players had to remember which order the lights flashed in.

SPIDER'S WEB

This spider's web game is great fun, climb in and out with everyone.

Difficulty: ⭐⭐⭐⭐⭐ **Players:** any number

You will need:
- lots of balls of wool
- small presents

1 Prepare this game before the party starts. Tie one end of a ball of wool to each small present – one per player. Hide the presents.

2 Unwind each ball of wool around table legs, door handles, staircases and so on, to make a giant criss-crossed spider's web.

3 As the guests arrive, give each of them the end of one ball of wool. They have to crawl in and out of the web, under furniture and around each other, winding up their wool as they go, to get to their prize.

Bet You Can't! tie different coloured lengths of wool together, so that each person's start and finish colour is different — there can be no cheating that way!

The winner is... everyone who finds their present!

DRAMA SCHOOL

What are you acting? Give us a clue!
Your friends must guess from what you do.

Difficulty: ⭐⭐⭐⭐⭐ **Players:** 3 or more

1 Players take it in turns to stand in front of everyone else and silently act the name of a book, TV programme or a film, for the other players to guess.

2 No speaking is allowed, except from those guessing. Play until someone guesses correctly, and then swap actors.

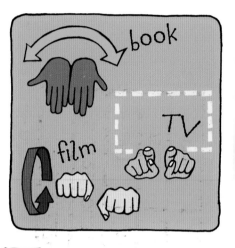

Did You Know?

You can make a '+' sign with two fingers to mean 'and', and a 'T' sign with two fingers to mean 'the'.

3 You can use the mimes above to start with, to show if you are acting a book, TV programme or a film.

The winner is... anyone who has fun!